SAN PABLO

GEORGIA

PATTIE STECHSCHULTE

Consultants

MELISSA N. MATUSEVICH, PH.D.

Curriculum and Instruction Specialist
Blacksburg, Virginia

THE CHILDREN'S SERVICES QUADRANT COUNCIL

Office of Public Library Services
A Unit of the Board of Regents of the University System of Georgia

CHILDREN'S PRESS®

A DIVISION OF SCHOLASTIC INC.

New York • Toronto • London • Auckland • Sydney • Mexico City
New Delhi • Hong Kong • Danbury, Connecticut

Georgia is in the southeastern part of the United States and is bordered by South Carolina, North Carolina, Tennessee, Alabama, Florida, and the Atlantic Ocean.

Project Editor: Lewis K. Parker
Art Director: Marie O'Neill
Photo Researcher: Marybeth Kavanagh
Design: Robin West, Ox and Company, Inc.
Page 6 map and recipe art: Susan Hunt Yule
All other maps: XNR Productions, Inc.

Library of Congress Cataloging-in-Publication Data
Stechschulte, Pattie.
      Georgia / by Pattie Stechschulte.
         p. cm—(From sea to shining sea)
      Includes bibliographical references (p.) and index.
      ISBN 0-516-22311-9
1. Georgia—Juvenile literature. [1. Georgia.] I. Title. II. From sea to shining sea (Series)

F286.3 .S74 2001
975.8—dc21   00-069388

TABLE of CONTENTS

CHAPTER

Georgia has many exciting things to do such as rafting on the Chattahoochee River.

Georgia has two nicknames. Sometimes Georgia is called "The Peach State" because so many peach trees grow in the state. Georgia is also called the "Empire State of the South" because of the state's size. Georgia is the largest state east of the Mississippi River.

Whatever Georgia's nickname, the state seems like several states wrapped up into one. Georgia's landscape has waterfalls, a huge swamp, fertile farmland, and golden ocean beaches. Millions of people visit Georgia every year. Some people hike through the mountains in the north. Some vacation on the beaches of Georgia's barrier islands. Others tour plantations and Civil War battlefields.

Georgia has always played an important part in our nation's history. It was the thirteenth original colony. Later, gunfire riddled its northern mountains when Confederate troops defended Georgia soil. Dr. Martin Luther King Jr. led the Civil Rights movement from Georgia. In modern times, people have moved to Georgia for the warm climate and the opportunity for work.

What comes to mind when you think of Georgia?
* Southern mansions with tall pillars
* Huge swamps with alligators and herons
* Stone Mountain with the sculptures of Jefferson Davis, Stonewall Jackson, and Robert E. Lee
* Sites where Civil War battles took place
* President Jimmy Carter serving his country
* Peach trees loaded with peaches
* People enjoying the sandy beaches
* The huge bottle of Coca-Cola at the World of Coca-Cola building

Georgia is a beautiful southern state. The state's history lies on its riverbanks, its battlefields, and in its cities. This book will tell you about some of the people, places, and events that make Georgia special.

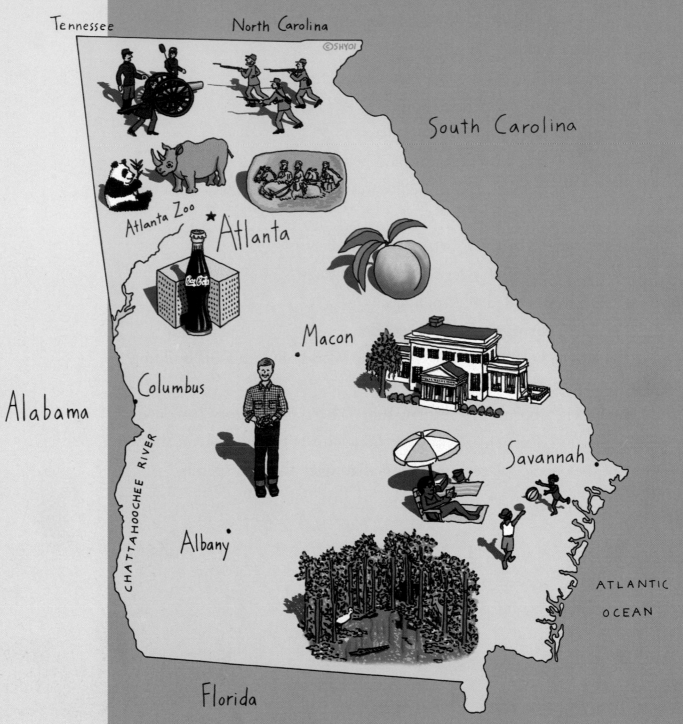

Tennessee

North Carolina

©SHYOI

South Carolina

Atlanta Zoo

★ Atlanta

Alabama

Columbus

Macon

CHATTAHOOCHEE RIVER

Albany

Savannah

ATLANTIC
OCEAN

Florida

CHAPTER TWO

THE LAND OF GEORGIA

The largest state east of the Mississippi River, Georgia is located in the southeast. The state's mountainous northern border is shared by Tennessee and North Carolina. The Savannah River and a few lakes make up the eastern border with South Carolina. The Atlantic Ocean washes up on the southeast coastline and Florida is to the south. The Chattahoochee River forms half the border with Alabama to the west.

Georgia stretches from the mountains in the north, across farmland in the middle, and to beaches on the Atlantic Ocean. More than half of the state is covered with trees. Georgia's huge landscape is made up of many sections. The geographic regions range from the Appalachian Plateau in the north to the coastal plains in the south.

This breathtaking scene can be found in the Chattahoochee National Forest.

Dawn arrives on Jekyll Island.

EXTRA! EXTRA!

Georgia's highest point is part of the Blue Ridge Mountains. Brasstown Bald is 4,784 feet (1,458 meters) above sea level. A "bald" is a mountaintop with a grassy peak. Scientists have no idea how these grassy, rounded knobs occur.

FIND OUT MORE

The Cherokee have a legend about Brasstown Bald, which they called Mount Enotah. According to the legend, long ago the world was covered with water. One family survived the flood. They put two of each kind of animal in a ship and sailed on the water until they struck land. The ship landed on Mount Enotah. What are some legends or stories about geographical features in your area?

At the extreme northwestern corner of the state is the Appalachian Plateau. It consists of two flat-topped mountains that drop into the Lookout and Chickamauga valleys. Some of the largest cliffs drop the length of a football field.

The Ridge and Valley region covers the northwest section of the state. It stretches from Atlanta to Chattanooga. This region is made up of narrow ridges next to open valleys.

The Blue Ridge Mountains are part of the Appalachian Mountain chain. They extend into northern Georgia. They are the oldest mountains in the world.

Just west of the Blue Ridge Mountains is Amicalola Falls, which means "tumbling waters" in the Cherokee language. These falls are the highest waterfalls in Georgia. They drop 729 feet (222 m). A little farther east are the steep granite cliffs of Tallulah Gorge. These cliffs plunge 1,000 feet (305 m). The two-mile valley has five waterfalls.

The second largest region in Georgia is the Piedmont region. Half of the population lives in this region. It has green rolling hills and red clay. The Piedmont starts at the mountains, goes through Atlanta, and ends at the Fall Line in central Georgia. The

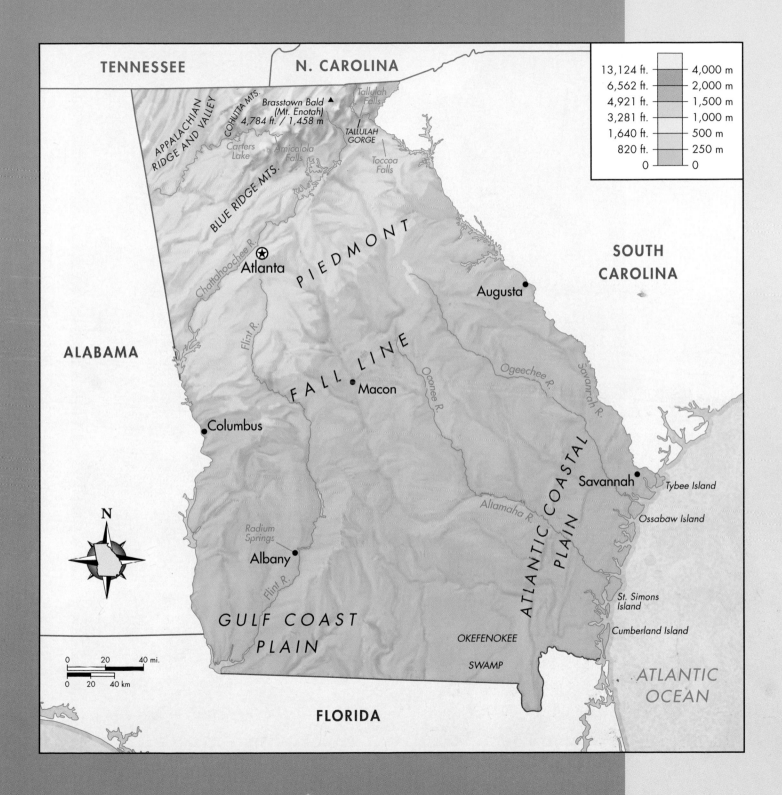

TENNESSEE

N. CAROLINA

APPALACHIAN RIDGE AND VALLEY

COHUTTA MTS.

Brasstown Bald
(Mt. Enotah)
4,784 ft. / 1,458 m

Tallulah Falls

TALLULAH GORGE

Carters Lake

Amicalola Falls

BLUE RIDGE MTS.

Toccoa Falls

P I E D M O N T

Chattahoochee R.

Atlanta

SOUTH CAROLINA

Augusta

Flint R.

F A L L   L I N E

Macon

Oconee R.

Ogeechee R.

Savannah R.

ALABAMA

Columbus

A T L A N T I C   C O A S T A L   P L A I N

Savannah

Tybee Island

Altamaha R.

Ossabaw Island

N

Radium Springs

Albany

Flint R.

St. Simons Island

Cumberland Island

GULF COAST PLAIN

OKEFENOKEE

SWAMP

ATLANTIC OCEAN

0   20   40 mi.
0   20   40 km

FLORIDA

13,124 ft.	4,000 m
6,562 ft.	2,000 m
4,921 ft.	1,500 m
3,281 ft.	1,000 m
1,640 ft.	500 m
820 ft.	250 m
0	0

Toccoa Falls is one of many fascinating waterfalls in Georgia.

foothills become smaller near the Fall Line, and the ground changes from rock to sand. Waterfalls and rapids formed at the Fall Line because water easily cuts through sand.

The Gulf Coastal Plain and Atlantic Coastal Plain region represents over half of the southern part of the state. This area has many farms where peanuts, peaches, and pecans grow. Pine trees are also grown here as lumber to make paper and tar.

The Atlantic Ocean coastline of Georgia is only 100 miles (161 km) long, but with islands and bays there are more than 2,000 miles (3219 km) of beaches. A line of barrier islands protects the mainland from hurricanes and ocean storms.

FIND OUT MORE

The Appalachian Trail starts in north Georgia and ends in Maine. Every year, thousands of people hike this trail. Hikers usually walk eighteen to twenty-four miles a day. How long might it take a person to walk the 2,158-mile (3,473-km) Appalachian Trail?

CLIMATE

In the summer, Georgia can feel like a tropical jungle. With high humidity and temperatures that reach just above 100°F (30°C), people depend on air conditioning and fans. The highest temperature recorded reached a scorching 113°F (45°C) on May 27, 1978, at Greenville. The winters are very mild and snow rarely falls south of the Appalachian Mountain region. January 27, 1940, was a cold day in Floyd County. On that day the temperature dipped to −17°F (−27°C), setting a record low.

The weather is cooler in the mountains. During the winter, mountain temperatures can fall to a little lower than 40°F (4°C). Snow may fall in the mountains. Nearly 80 inches (203 centimeters) of rain falls in the mountains each year.

Tornadoes occur in every part of the state during the spring. The worst tornado hit in Gainesville in 1936. This tornado killed 203 people and destroyed more than 750 homes. A recent tornado in February 2000 left 19 people dead and more than 100 injured in southwestern Georgia.

Five hurricanes have struck the Georgia coast in the last hundred years. However, many storms can cause damage after they hit the Florida and Carolina coasts. In 1994, Tropical Storm Alberto caused severe flooding in Georgia. Thirty-three people were killed and fifty-five counties were declared disaster areas.

RIVERS AND OTHER WATERWAYS

Every river in Georgia begins in the state or on the border. No rivers flow into the state, only out. The two major rivers are the Chattahoochee and Savannah.

The Chattahoochee River, nicknamed "the Hooch," is formed from the runoff in the Blue Ridge Mountains in northeast Georgia. It winds 436 miles (702 km) through the state and into Florida. This river becomes the Apalachicola River in Florida. The Chattahoochee River forms the boundary between Georgia and Alabama from West Point, Georgia, to the Florida border. Atlanta and Columbus, Georgia's two largest cities, lie on the banks of the Chattahoochee. Dams on the river created Lake Lanier and also provide Atlanta's water supply.

The longest river to flow through Georgia is the Savannah. The Savannah River flows 341 miles (549 km) from Lake Hartwell to the Atlantic Ocean. It marks the border between Georgia and South Carolina. Many nature and wildlife preserves, such as the Tuckahoe Wildlife Management Area and the Savannah National Wildlife Refuge, border the river. Wild boar, deer, ducks, geese, alligators, and fish live in these areas. A dam on the Savannah created Clarks Hill Lake, also known as Lake Thurmond, which is one of Georgia's largest artificial, or manmade, lakes.

The Altamaha River system starts with the Ocmulgee and Oconee Rivers. Where the Ocmulgee and Oconee join in central Georgia near

These people are enjoying the water and beach at Lake Lanier.

The Okefenokee Swamp is a mysterious place.

Lumber City, the Altamaha begins its slow trip to the Atlantic Ocean. This is a wilderness area. During the days of the lumber camps, logs floated down the Altamaha to Darien to be cut into boards.

To the southeast, the Altamaha creates a wide delta. This is a broad, flat plain. The Altamaha is a tidal river and its tides affect the river's height up to forty miles inland from the Atlantic Ocean. The flood plain is about 12 miles (19 km) wide. It provides rich soil for growing rice.

The Golden Isles, a group of islands, form a line between the Altamaha River's end and the Atlantic Ocean. Big Hammock Natural Area is formed by the odd sand ridges that mark Georgia's lower coastal plain. Visitors find a mixture of plant and wildlife, including prickly pear cactus, spikemoss, and scrub pine. Armadillos and gopher tortoises also find the marshy region to their liking. Hidden in the swamps are eastern diamondback rattlers and indigo snakes.

The Okefenokee Swamp is the second largest freshwater swamp in the country. The swamp covers more than 650 square miles (1,683 sq km). It is a national wildlife refuge protected by the U.S. Government.

This swamp is a strange, eerie place. Native Americans named this place "the land of the trembling earth." The land in the swamp is not land at all. What looks like land is actually peat bogs floating on the surface of the swamp water. Peat is a sponge-like layer of soil created from decayed and dried plants. It is very difficult to walk on peat. Trying to walk through the swamp is like stepping on shaky ground—the "trembling earth."

Huge 80-foot (24-m) tall cypress trees loom over the swamp water. Below these huge trees are wax myrtle, black gum, red maple, and bay trees. Bamboo and several kinds of berry bushes can be found. Among the more unusual plants is the pitcher plant. This is a plant that eats insects. It lures insects into the center of its pretty flower where the insects become stuck, and then the plant eats its prey. There are thirty-five kinds of snakes in the swamp, and five are deadly. These include the black water moccasin or cottonmouth, the coral snake, and rattlesnakes. Alligators share the water's edge with alligator snapping turtles—large freshwater turtles that can weigh up to 150 pounds (68 kg).

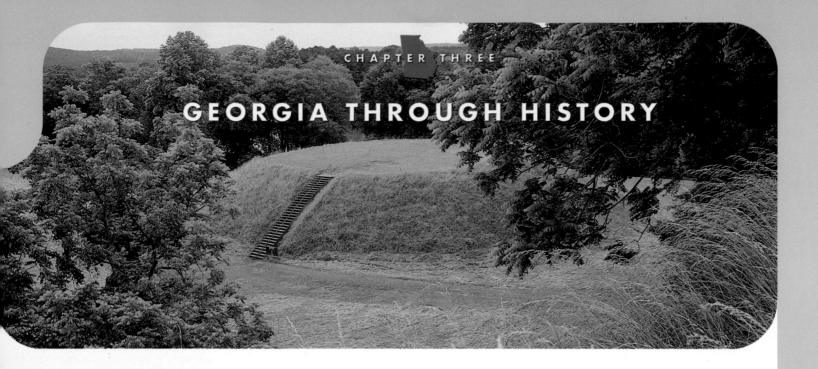

CHAPTER THREE

GEORGIA THROUGH HISTORY

Etowah Indian Mounds are located near Cartersville. One of the mounds is the largest in the southern Appalachians. It is 63 feet (19 m) high and covers 3 acres.

Millions of years ago, water covered almost all of Georgia. In recent years, farmers on the Coastal Plains have uncovered fossils of shark teeth when plowing their land. One fossil was from a Carcharodon, an ancient shark, which had teeth six inches long. This creature was 50 feet (15 m) long and lived about 20 million years ago.

The first humans came into Georgia about 12,000 years ago. They were hunters who probably followed herds of large animals for food.

About 3,000 years ago, Native Americans lived in what is now Georgia. At first, they moved from place to place, living along the coast or beside rivers. They hunted deer in the forests and collected shellfish. Over a period of time, they moved farther inland and built villages. These people are called the Mississippians or Mound Builders. They farmed, made ceramic pots, traded with other tribes, and built temple mounds. The mounds are more than 60 feet (18 m) tall with flat tops.

The tribe's chief priest lived in huts on top of the mounds and Native Americans buried important people inside the mounds. The Mound Builders left huge mounds at Etowah and Ocmulgee.

By 1500 three Native American tribes lived in Georgia. The Cherokees lived north of the Chattahoochee River. The Creeks lived south of the river into Alabama. The Seminole nation stretched into south Georgia from Florida.

EARLY EXPLORERS

The Spanish were the first Europeans to explore what is now Georgia. Hernando de Soto conducted the first major exploration of Georgia in 1540. He led more than six hundred soldiers looking for gold. As they traveled through the southeast, they encountered many Native American villages. Some of the tribes were friendly, offering shelter and food. Other tribes hid from the Spanish soldiers.

During their journey through Georgia, the Spanish ran out of food. The troops stole corn from the villages and sometimes killed or took the natives as slaves. The Spanish never found any gold. Their brutality against the Native Americans created distrust. The explorers also brought European diseases to the natives. Thousands of Cherokee and Creek died from diseases such as smallpox.

Spanish interest in the area of Georgia continued when Catholic priests from Florida built two churches on Jekyll Island and St. Simons Island in 1566. At that time, Spain controlled Florida and wanted to establish an empire to the north. They called this land Guale. They provided the churches with supplies and protection. Over the next hundred years, the priests taught Christianity to thousands of Native Americans. Spanish missions were built along the coast and as far inland as the Chattahoochee River.

During this time, the British colony of South Carolina to the north grew in size and strength. English settlers began moving into Georgia. The Spanish had a hard time maintaining their control in Guale. Pirates also attacked and robbed the missions, sometimes killing the priests. By 1695, the Spanish priests deserted the missions and returned to Florida.

England wanted to include the area of Georgia as part of its colony of South Carolina. In 1721, colonists from South Carolina built Fort King George across the Savannah River in southeast Georgia. The fort was abandoned by 1727.

James Oglethorpe founded the colony of Georgia.

JAMES OGLETHORPE AND THE TRUSTEES

In the early 1730s, James Oglethorpe, a wealthy Englishman and a member of England's Parliament, wanted to start a colony in the Americas. He wanted to give poor people a fresh start by taking them to the colony. Oglethorpe also wanted people of different religions to come to the colony. The official church of England is Anglican. People of different religions were often mistreated. He wanted the new colony to be a refuge, or safe place, for these people.

Other Englishmen also hoped that the new colony would be able to produce spices, wine, and silk. These products were very expensive because they had to be brought from other countries. These men believed that silk and wine would be cheaper if they were made in the colonies.

At the same time, colonists living in South Carolina wanted protection from the Spanish armies in Florida. Oglethorpe asked King George II for permission to start a colony south of the Carolina colonies. In 1732, the king signed a charter. This official document gave Oglethorpe and a group of twenty-one men called "trustees" permission to start and govern a colony.

Thirty-five families sailed for the new land, which became Georgia. It was named for King George II. The colonists were given free passage, fifty acres of land to farm, and enough supplies to last one year. There were only three rules—slavery and rum were not allowed, and no one could own land. The land they farmed didn't belong to them.

On a February morning in 1733, Oglethorpe and 116 colonists established a settlement at Yamacraw Bluff, which later became known

as Savannah. High ground provided trees for houses and good soil for farming. Oglethorpe signed a treaty with the Creeks for land. The natives regularly brought food and supplies to trade with colonists.

Savannah was the first planned city in the colonies. Oglethorpe designed the plan. There were many squares containing houses around a public area or park. People would do trading or hold public meetings in the square. He also started a ten-acre garden. Colonists planted seeds and trees to see which ones would grow the best in Georgia soil. The first peach tree was planted here.

The colonists faced a problem with their crops. They could not grow the mulberry trees used to make silk or the grape vines to make wine. They soon learned that rice and indigo were the best crops to grow. The indigo plant was used to make blue dye for clothes.

The trustees brought more settlers into Georgia after Savannah was founded. Some of the people were from Germany, Scotland, and Switzerland. They usually stayed in Savannah for a few weeks after their ocean voyage. Then the trustees would take them to another area and help them start a new settlement.

In 1736, Philip Georg Friedrich von Reck traveled from Germany to help found the city of Ebenezer. In his diary, he reported, "The climate is warm and hot in the months of June, July, and August. On the other hand, the nights are very cold. The sandy soil is most fertile in winter,

EXTRA! EXTRA!

During this time, slavery existed in the colonies. People were captured in Africa and then sold as slaves in the colonies. Slaves were treated as property that could be bought and sold. They did the hard work on farms, and could be punished by their owners for not working or for trying to escape.

This woman carries sheaves on a rice plantation.

when it is wettest, and very usable for garden crops. The heavy soil is good for corn and all kinds of grain. The marshes are the best for rice cultivation, which is the most productive and useful crop here."

At this time, England controlled the eastern portion of the country. The French had settlements in the north, west, and south. Armies of the two countries had been fighting for control over North America since 1689. In 1739, Spain joined the fight and declared war on England.

Oglethorpe expected Spain to attack Georgia, so he built forts along the coast. Oglethorpe was right. In 1742, Spain invaded St. Simons Island. Oglethorpe and a small army launched a surprise attack on Spanish troops in the marshes. Because the colonists were hidden in the marshes, the Spaniards did not know how large the army was. The Spanish retreated back to Florida. This fight was called the Battle of Bloody Marsh because of the large amount of bloodshed in the swamp.

By 1750 about 5,000 people lived in Georgia. Colonists convinced the trustees to allow slavery and alcohol. People were also allowed to own and sell land. In 1752, the trustees gave up control of Georgia. It became a royal colony ruled by a governor, who was appointed by the king of England.

THE AMERICAN REVOLUTION AND STATEHOOD

Between 1754 and 1763, France and England fought the French and Indian War. It was a war to decide which country would control most of North America. No large battles occurred in Georgia. All of the fighting

American Revolutionary soldiers prepare for a battle.

was in the north. England won the war, but borrowed a lot of money to do so. To help raise money, England decided to tax the colonists, charging them extra money for certain products. This angered many people.

As a new colony, most Georgians were still loyal to England. However, a group of rebels formed in 1765 called the Sons of Liberty. They led public protests against the new taxes in every colony, including Georgia. These leaders became known as patriots. They asked the king several times to stop the taxes, but he refused.

Finally, seeking freedom from England, the colonists fought the American Revolution (1775–1783). English troops captured Savannah in December 1778 and soon controlled the rest of the state. In 1782,

FAMOUS FIRSTS

- First silk factory in the United States was in Savannah in 1751
- First state college to award degrees to women was the Georgia Female College (Wesleyan College) in Macon in 1839
- First African-American U.S. Congressman to give a speech before the U.S. House of Representatives was Georgia's representative Jefferson Franklin Long in 1871
- First Girl Scout meeting was in Juliette Low's Savannah home in 1912
- First telephone call across the continental United States was from Jekyll Island to San Francisco (1915)
- First state to allow eighteen-year-olds to vote in 1943

General Anthony Wayne led American troops into Georgia to take back control. The English troops were defeated and left Georgia. The war ended in 1783.

Georgia ratified the Constitution of the United States in 1788. This document contains the laws and beliefs for the new nation. Georgia became the fourth state to join what was now the United States of America.

KING COTTON

Times changed dramatically for Georgia in 1793. That year, Eli Whitney invented the cotton gin while visiting a plantation near Savannah. Whitney's machine forever changed the way cotton was harvested. Before this invention, seeds were removed from cotton by hand, which was a long and difficult process. It would take a slave a full day to remove the seeds from one pound of cotton. Using the cotton gin, which removed seeds by machine, a slave could process about fifty pounds of cotton in one day. In 1791, farmers produced 1,000 bales. By 1800, the number had increased to 20,000 bales.

Cotton grew very well in the southern and middle part of Georgia. In fact, cotton replaced most other crops. It became the richest crop of the South, nicknamed "King Cotton." Now cotton planters could afford to buy more slaves. They bought thousands of slaves to do the hard work. Many people moved to Georgia and the population soared to more than 250,000 by 1810.

In 1795 some companies tricked state legislators into selling them land in west Georgia. They bought 35 million acres for about a penny an acre. The companies then sold that same land at a huge profit. Once people found out about it, the companies were forced to give the land back to the state. This swindle was called the Yazoo Land Fraud after the Yazoo River flowing through the land. Afterward, the state held a land lottery. They sold almost all of the land to about 100,000 people for seven cents an acre.

Eli Whitney (1765–1825) invented the cotton gin. His invention caused a huge increase in cotton production.

This drawing shows slaves using a cotton gin.

Thousands of acres of forests were cut down to make room for new cotton fields. As more people moved into Georgia and more land was used for farming, the Creeks were forced out of Georgia. By 1827, they gave up their land to the government. The only remaining Native Americans in Georgia were the Cherokees. The tribe had established an independent nation in north Georgia.

The Cherokees had adopted the ways of the European settlers. They wore the same clothes as the colonists and lived in houses. Most Cherokees had accepted the Christian religion. They wrote a constitution very similar to the U.S. Constitution. From their capital in New Echota, they printed the nation's only Native American newspaper—*The Cherokee Phoenix*.

It created a big problem for the Cherokees when gold was discovered on Cherokee land in 1828. Chaos erupted as settlers from other states rushed onto Cherokee land to dig for gold.

Benjamin Parks was one of the first people to find gold. He found a gold nugget when he was deer hunting. As he kicked a stone, he noticed, "The stone was some-

The first gold strike in the United States occurred in Georgia.

thing like that of an egg yolk. A deep rich yellow hue. It was gold."

Most gold seekers practiced deposit mining. They dipped pans or pots into the soil of the riverbank. Then they picked or strained out the gold dust or nuggets. Some people dug caves in the mountains with drills in hopes of finding even more gold.

The Cherokees didn't want gold prospectors on their land. They went to court to stop them from mining there. Following a long court battle, the U.S. Supreme Court sided with the Cherokees in 1832, but President Andrew Jackson did not support their decision. A few years earlier, in 1830, he had succeeded in passing a law called the Indian Removal Act. This law called for all Native Americans to be moved beyond the Mississippi River to what is now Oklahoma.

In 1833, Georgia held a land lottery to divide up the Cherokee nation. In hopes of finding peace, a small band of Cherokees signed the Treaty of New Echota. They sold their land for $5 million.

In 1838, four thousand U.S. troops came into Georgia to immediately remove the Cherokee and bring them to Oklahoma. A few Cherokees escaped and hid in the mountains of North Carolina.

The Cherokees were not allowed to take clothes or blankets. Most of them did not have any coats or shoes. They started their 1,000-mile (1609-km) journey in October in wagons with no shelter. The soldiers did not provide them with enough food for the trip. They had to beg the soldiers to hunt for food along the way. Many became sick from hunger and the cold. More than 4,000 Cherokee died on the 116-day trip to Oklahoma. The Cherokees call this journey "Nunna-da-ul-tsun-yi," which means "The Trail of Tears."

RAILROAD CONNECTIONS

Georgia continued to prosper in the 1830s. The state built and owned the Western & Atlantic Railroad to connect DeKalb County with Chattanooga, Tennessee. The southern end of the railroad in Georgia was a little town called Terminus. In 1845 the name was changed to Marthasville and in 1849 to Atlanta. In 1868 Atlanta became the state capital.

This railroad gave Georgia a track directly to the Tennessee River. The Tennessee flowed into the Ohio and then into the Mississippi River. Now farmers had a way to transport cotton and sugar to markets in the North. By 1860 Georgia had 1,400 miles (2,253 km) of rail and the best system of railroads in the South.

SLAVERY IN GEORGIA

By the 1850s Georgia planters were very dependent on slavery. In 1790, about 30,000 African-American slaves lived in Georgia. By 1860 the number of slaves had climbed to 460,000.

Most slaves lived in wooden shacks on their owners' farms and plantations. Slaves cooked at a fireplace, which also provided warmth for the

cabin. Most slaves owned two changes of clothes—one for summer, and one for winter.

Life in the northern states was much different. In the northern states, slavery was illegal. There were many factories, mills, and businesses where people were paid wages for their work. In the South, where there were not many factories, most people worked in farming. The main crop was cotton. Many Southern planters argued that their farms could not exist without slave labor, which was legal in the South.

This drawing shows a row of cabins where slaves lived.

Abraham Lincoln was elected U.S. President in 1860. Before he was elected, he had promised that slavery would not be allowed in the new territories and new states. He also said that the United States could not continue to exist as it was—half slave and half free.

Leaders in the Southern states did not want to end slavery. They decided to secede, or leave, the United States and form their own country where slavery would be legal. Georgia joined other Southern states to form the Confederate States of America in January of 1861. The other states were Texas, Arkansas, Alabama, Florida, Louisiana, Mississippi, South Carolina, North Carolina, Tennessee, and Virginia. Jefferson Davis became president of the Confederacy. Alexander Stephens, a U.S. Congressman from Georgia, became vice president.

THE CIVIL WAR

The Civil War (1861–1865) started on April 12, 1861, when Confederate troops fired on Fort Sumter in Charleston's harbor in South Carolina. Georgia played a very important part in the war. About 125,000 men volunteered to serve in the Confederate army. Georgia farms supplied food and clothing needed by Confederate troops. Using Georgia's excellent system of railroads, supplies were sent out from Atlanta.

The first attack on Georgia came from the sea. Union troops landed on Cockspur Island and captured Fort Pulaski. They blocked the Savannah River so no ships could deliver supplies to Savannah.

The first major land battle was fought in late 1863. The Battle of

Chickamauga was a two-day battle in the mountains near the northwest corner of the state. Union troops wanted to gain control of the railroad near Chattanooga, but the Confederate troops defeated the Union forces. It was one of the bloodiest battles of the war. About 16,000 Union and 18,000 Confederate troops died. It was the last major victory for the Confederacy.

In May 1864, Union General William T. Sherman received orders to invade Georgia. He had an army of about 100,000 troops located near Chattanooga. They slowly pushed 62,000 Confederate troops

Many Union and Confederate soldiers died at the battle of Chickamauga.

south. These troops lost more than a dozen battles before retreating to Atlanta. Sherman's army fired cannons on the city for forty days before the Confederate army left. On September 1, 1864, Sherman claimed the city of Atlanta.

This painting shows General Sherman on horseback.

Back in Washington, President Lincoln was very happy when he heard the news. He was in the middle of the 1864 presidential election. The war had been going on for three years and many people wanted it to end. With the capture of Atlanta, people believed the end of the war was near. People regained faith in Lincoln and reelected him.

Sherman and his troops stayed in Atlanta for two months. When the Union army left, soldiers burned every warehouse and destroyed the railroads. He never meant to destroy the entire city, but the fire raged out of control. In the end, only about four hundred homes were left standing.

Sherman headed south toward Savannah with 60,000 troops on November 15. His goal was to destroy every farm and railroad track from Atlanta to the Atlantic Ocean. Georgia would no longer be able to supply food to the Confederate army. This campaign was called Sherman's "March to the Sea."

The Union soldiers formed a column that was forty miles (64 km) wide. Soldiers struck every farm in their path, taking all the food they could carry. What they couldn't carry or eat, they burned, spoiled, or ruined. They burned farmhouses and plantation homes. After marching 300 miles, Sherman arrived at Savannah on December 21, 1864. The city surrendered without a shot being fired.

WHAT'S IN A NAME?

Many names of places in Georgia have interesting origins.

Name	Comes from or means
Atlanta	Western & Atlantic Railroad
Chickamauga	"the river of death" in Cherokee language
Lake Lanier	Georgia poet Sidney Lanier
Chattahoochee River	"painted rock," Creeks found material for war paint on the banks of the river
Okefenokee Swamp	"land of the trembling earth" in Seminole language

The Civil War ended when Confederate General Robert E. Lee agreed to peace terms on April 9, 1865, at Appomattox Courthouse, Virginia. About 25,000 Georgian soldiers died in the war.

RECONSTRUCTION

After the war, the divided nation entered a period called Reconstruction. This was a time of rebuilding. African-Americans were now free people. The Fourteenth Amendment to the U.S. Constitution gave them the right to vote.

The governments of the southern states were closed down. Military officers governed the states until elections could be held. In 1868 thirty-two African-Americans were elected to Georgia's House of Representatives as Republicans. The state of Georgia was readmitted to the Union in 1870. When Georgia became a state, new elections were held. The Democratic party regained control of the state government, and the newly elected officials quickly removed all the African-American representatives.

Many white Southerners also wanted to limit the rights of African-Americans. The state legislature passed Jim Crow laws in the 1880s. These laws separated white people and African-Americans. African-Americans were not allowed to use the same public restrooms, attend the same public schools, eat in the same restaurants, or sit in the same buses or trains as white people. African-Americans started their own churches, schools, restaurants, and clubs. To make it difficult for

African-Americans to vote, the state legislature passed a poll tax. People had to pay the tax in order to vote. Many African-Americans could not pay the tax and so were not allowed to vote.

Some Southerners formed a secret society called the Ku Klux Klan. They disguised themselves by wearing white robes and masks. At night Ku Klux Klan members spread terror by attacking the homes and businesses of African-Americans, then beating and sometimes killing them. From 1880 to 1930, about 439 African-Americans were lynched (hanged) throughout Georgia.

After the Civil War ended, many African-Americans stayed on the same farms where they had once been slaves. They became sharecroppers or tenant farmers. They made agreements with the landowners allowing them to farm the land in exchange for a share of the profits when the crops were harvested.

Many African-Americans were forced to become sharecroppers or tenant farmers.

Many landowners took advantage of the African-Americans. Landowners lent sharecroppers money to buy seed, tools, and mules. When the crop was harvested, the landowners would subtract how much money the sharecropper had borrowed from the profits. Sharecroppers often ended up owing money to landowners. For many African-Americans, this became a new form of slavery.

A NEW CENTURY

Atlanta hosted the 1895 Cotton States and International Exposition. There were about 6,000 exhibits, including the world's largest Ferris Wheel. About one million people attended the exposition. One of the speakers was Booker T. Washington. He was the son of

The boll weevil destroyed cotton crops throughout Georgia.

a former slave, and he ran an African-American school in Alabama called the Tuskegee Institute. He talked about how important it was for whites and African-Americans to work together. He stressed that the only way for African-Americans to get ahead was through education and hard work.

In 1914 World War I (1914–1918) broke out in Europe. Most of the fighting was along the border of France and Germany. The United States entered the war in April 1917. Ships were built in Savannah. About 100,000 soldiers from Georgia served in the war.

In 1914, a small insect called the boll weevil arrived in Georgia. The boll weevil had a terrible affect on cotton production. Female beetles would lay eggs inside the cotton bud, and when the eggs hatched, the insects ate the bud and destroyed the plant. Cotton production fell from

EXTRA! EXTRA!

Along with eighteen young girls, Juliette Low formed the Girl Guides in Savannah in 1912. Within a few years, the group had more than 5,000 members across the country and changed its name to the Girl Scouts of America. Today, it is the world's largest voluntary organization for girls.

over two million bales in 1918 to only 588,000 in 1923. Nearly two out of every ten farmers left their farms. They could no longer support their families by farming. Many farmers moved to Atlanta or farther north to find work in the cities. The remaining farmers started planting other crops, including peanuts and pine trees.

THE GREAT DEPRESSION AND WORLD WAR II

In 1929, the United States entered the Great Depression (1929–1939). A depression is a time when businesses do very poorly and many people are unemployed. In 1929 the stock market crashed and many companies lost a great deal of money. Throughout the country, banks closed and businesses shut down. About three out of every ten Americans was out of work. Farmers couldn't sell their crops. Many families were hungry and poor.

U.S. President Franklin D. Roosevelt tried to get people working again through a program called the New Deal. Many people found jobs working for the U.S. Government. People were hired to build bridges, roads, and buildings in Georgia. Government workers also taught about 250,000 African-Americans how to read and write.

World War II (1939–1945) ended the Great Depression. The United States joined forces with England, France, and the Soviet Union to fight Germany, Italy, and Japan. The army needed new ships and bombers. Factories in Georgia began to produce these items, bringing many new jobs to the state. The B-29 bomber plane was made in Marietta. Soldiers were trained at Fort Benning in Columbus. New ships were built at the shipyards in Savannah and Brunswick. Thousands of men and women were employed. More than 300,000 soldiers from Georgia served in the war.

AFTER WORLD WAR II

After the war, many companies moved to Georgia. Now more people were working in factories than on farms. Cities offered the companies low taxes and free buildings. Companies were attracted to Georgia because workers were paid less in the South. There were no unions in many southern states. Unions are organizations that help workers get higher pay and better working conditions. Lawmakers in Georgia passed laws to discourage unions from forming in the state.

In the 1950s change started for African-Americans. Many African-American leaders and many white people began what was known as

the Civil Rights movement. They believed African-Americans had the right to attend schools wherever they wanted. In May 1954, the U.S. Supreme Court ruled that it was wrong not to allow African-Americans to attend public schools.

A Georgia native, Dr. Martin Luther King Jr., became the leader of the movement. The group led peaceful protests throughout the southern states. One kind of protest was called a sit-in. Protestors would block entrances or sit on the floor of restaurants that did not serve African-Americans. They refused to move until their demands were met. Police officers arrested many protestors. However, the protests had an effect and laws began to change. By 1961 African-American children were attending public schools in Georgia along with white children.

Dr. King received the Nobel Peace Prize in 1964 for working toward equal rights for all Americans. In 1968 Dr. King traveled to Memphis, Tennessee to help city garbage workers get better pay. He was assassinated. However, many of his followers continued to fight for equality.

By the mid 1970s, African-Americans were elected to important offices in Georgia, including the U.S. Congress and the mayor of Atlanta. In 1976, Georgia Governor Jimmy Carter was elected president. He was the first president to appoint African-Americans to important jobs in the U.S. Government.

Since 1950 Georgia's population more than doubled from 3.5 million to over eight million in the year 2000. Today, most people live around Atlanta and other major cities. The population increase has caused some problems with the environment and traffic. Garbage and

opposite:
Governor Roy Barnes (right) and Cecil Alexander, the designer of the flag, hold the new state flag.

chemicals have been dumped into the Chattahoochee and Savannah Rivers. In fact, the Chattahoochee was named one of our nation's most endangered rivers and is now being cleaned and protected. Also, with so many cars on the road, Atlanta has an air pollution problem. People are encouraged to work at home. The state has also built carpool lanes on major highways.

In the last twenty years, many more large companies have moved to Atlanta. They have brought thousands of office jobs to the area. People from the north have migrated into the area looking for better jobs. Suburbs around Atlanta are filled with new houses, schools, shopping malls and roads.

Georgia received worldwide attention for twenty-one days in 1996, when Atlanta hosted the Summer Olympics. Visitors from around the world came to Georgia to see the hundreds of competitions. Millions more people watched the Olympics on television around the world.

Attention focused on Georgia again in 2001 with the adoption of a new state flag.

On January 30, 2001, the state Senate approved a new flag to replace one that many people said offended them. The old flag was basically the Confederate flag plus the state seal. The old state flag had been flown since 1956. The new flag pictures the Confederate flag along with a series of four other historical flags.

The adoption of a new state flag followed months of discussion. During the debate over the flag, the Sons of Confederate Veterans presented a petition to the state legislature. The petition was in favor of keeping the old flag and was signed by about 52,000 flag supporters. However, members of the National Association for the Advancement of Colored People (NAACP) and members of other civil rights organizations viewed the flag as a representation of slavery. In the end, Governor Roy Barnes signed the law that adopted the new flag. He said, "This is not about destroying heritage. This is about being unified as one people."

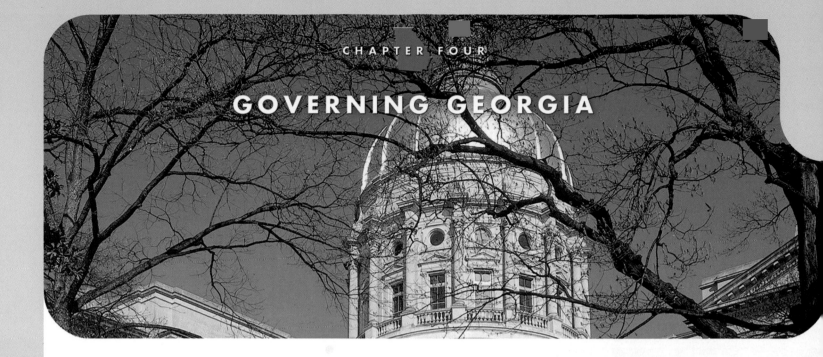

CHAPTER FOUR

GOVERNING GEORGIA

Georgia's first constitution was adopted during the American Revolutionary War in 1777. Since then, there have been a total of ten constitutions. The constitution had to be updated as the state grew and laws changed. The newest constitution was adopted in 1982.

The government of Georgia is set up like the U.S. Government. Georgia's government has three branches—the legislative, the executive, and the judicial. Each branch has a different function but no single branch is more powerful than any other.

The capitol building is noted for its gold dome.

LEGISLATIVE BRANCH

The Georgia legislature is called the General Assembly. It is made up of two groups—the Senate and the House of Representatives. Its main responsibility is to make laws for the state.

43

Members of the Georgia House of Representatives discuss an important matter.

The General Assembly meets every year from January to March for forty days. Each state senator and state representative is elected to two-year terms. Currently, there are 56 members of the Senate and 180 members in the House of Representatives.

Each year the senators and representatives meet to debate and pass laws. They pass laws to educate preschoolers, to protect the environment, and to build new roads, among other things. The General Assembly also controls how much money is spent by the government.

EXECUTIVE BRANCH

The executive branch carries out the laws. The head of the executive branch is the governor. The governor is elected every four years and can only be elected twice. Once the legislature passes a bill, it is the governor's decision to either sign the bill into law or to veto it. The governor develops new programs that must be

GEORGIA STATE GOVERNMENT

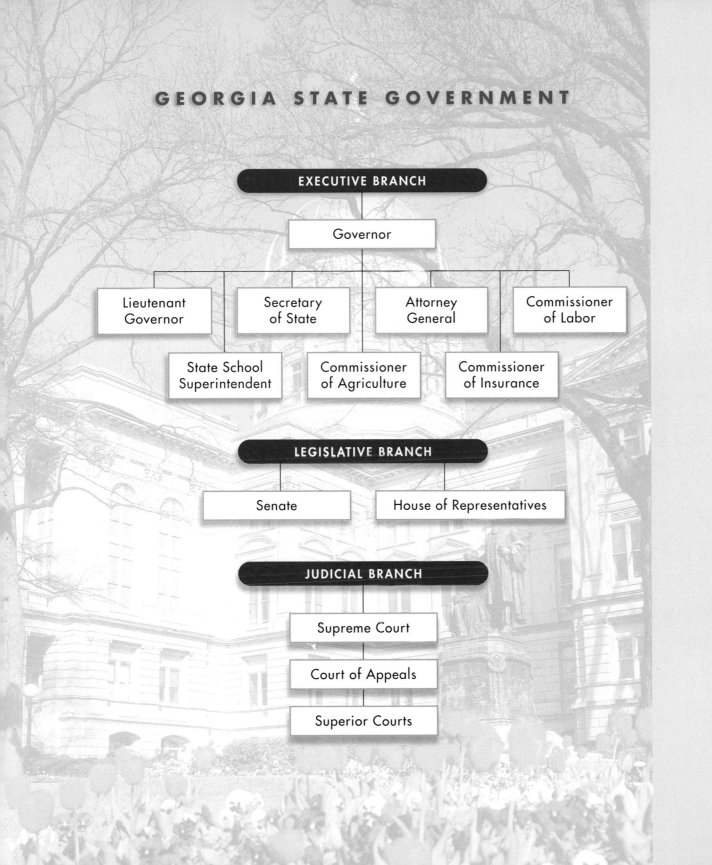

EXECUTIVE BRANCH

Governor

Lieutenant Governor

Secretary of State

Attorney General

Commissioner of Labor

State School Superintendent

Commissioner of Agriculture

Commissioner of Insurance

LEGISLATIVE BRANCH

Senate

House of Representatives

JUDICIAL BRANCH

Supreme Court

Court of Appeals

Superior Courts

approved by the General Assembly. They recommend how much money to spend in the state. They also choose people to run state agencies.

Along with the governor, eight other offices are elected. These offices are the attorney general, lieutenant governor, commissioner of labor, commissioner of agriculture, commissioner of insurance, secretary of state, state school superintendent, and public service commission. Because these offices are elected, they may have no loyalty to the governor. This can limit the governor's power.

JUDICIAL BRANCH

The judicial branch interprets the laws and is made up of the courts. There are many different courts in Georgia. Some courts deal with minor cases like traffic tickets. More important cases, like murder, are held in superior court. There is one court handling cases with children called juvenile court. The highest court of review is the Supreme Court. All judges are elected. Supreme Court justices and Court of Appeals judges serve for six years.

TAKE A TOUR OF ATLANTA, THE STATE CAPITAL

Atlanta has been the capital of Georgia since 1868. The city covers 132 square miles (342 sq km). The city is located in the northern area of the state. The Blue Ridge Mountains are not far from Atlanta and the Chattahoochee River borders Atlanta on its western side.

GEORGIA GOVERNORS

Name	Term	Name	Term
John Adam Treutlen	1777–1778*	Thomas H. Ruger	1868
John Houstoun	1778–1779*	Rufus B. Bullock	1868–1871
John Wereat	1779–1780*	Benjamin Conley	1871–1872
George Walton	1779–1780*	James M. Smith	1872–1877
Richard Howley	1780*	Alfred H. Colquitt	1877–1882
Stephen Heard	1780*	Alexander H. Stephens	1882–1883
Myrick Davies	1780–1781	James S. Boynton	1883
Nathan Brownson	1781–1782*	Henry D. McDaniel	1883–1886
John Martin	1782–1783*	John B. Gordon	1886–1890
Lyman Hall	1783–1784	William J. Northen	1890–1894
John Houstoun	1784–1785	William Y. Atkinson	1894–1898
Samuel Elbert	1785–1786	Allen D. Candler	1898–1902
Edward Telfair	1786–1787	Joseph M. Terrell	1902–1907
George Mathews	1787–1788	Hoke Smith	1907–1909
George Handley	1788–1789	Joseph M. Brown	1909–1911
George Walton	1789–1790	Hoke Smith	1911
Edward Telfair	1790–1793	John M. Slaton	1911–1912
George Mathews	1793–1796	Joseph M. Brown	1912–1913
Jared Irwin	1796–1798	John M. Slaton	1913–1915
James Jackson	1798–1801	Nathaniel E. Harris	1915–1917
David Emanuel	1801	Hugh M. Dorsey	1917–1921
Josiah Tattnall, Jr.	1801–1802	Thomas W. Hardwick	1921–1923
John Milledge	1802–1806	Clifford M. Walker	1923–1927
Jared Irwin	1806–1809	Lamartine Hardman	1927–1931
David B. Mitchell	1809–1813	Richard B. Russell, Jr.	1931–1933
Peter Early	1813–1815	Eugene Talmadge	1933–1937
David B. Mitchell	1815–1817	Eurith D. Rivers	1937–1941
William Rabun	1817–1819	Eugene Talmadge	1941–1943
Mathew Talbot	1819	Ellis G. Arnall	1943–1947
John Clark	1819–1823	Herman E. Talmadge	1947
George M. Troup	1823–1827	Melvin E. Thompson	1947–1948
John Forsyth	1827–1829	Herman E. Talmadge	1948–1955
George R. Gilmer	1829–1831	S. Marvin Griffin	1955–1959
Wilson Lumpkin	1831–1835	S. Ernest Vandiver, Jr.	1959–1963
William Schley	1835–1837	Carl E. Sanders	1963–1967
George R. Gilmer	1837–1839	Lester G. Maddox	1967–1971
Charles J. McDonald	1839–1843	James E. Carter	1971–1975
George W. Crawford	1843–1847	George Busbee	1975–1983
George W.B. Towns	1847–1851	Joe Frank Harris	1983–1991
Howell Cobb	1851–1853	Zell Miller	1991–1999
Herschel V. Johnson	1853–1857	Roy Barnes	1999–
Joseph E. Brown	1857–1865**		
James Johnson	1865**		
Charles J. Jenkins	1865–1868		

*Revolutionary War governors
**Confederate state governors

Kennesaw Mountain
National Battlefield Park

White Water
Theme Park

Six Flags
Over Georgia

Atlanta History
Center

Margaret Mitchell
House & Museum

Centennial
Olympic Park

Atlanta Botanical Gardens/
Piedmont Park

SciTrek
Museum

CNN Center

Jimmy Carter
Library & Museum

Fernbank Museum of
Natural History

World of Coca-Cola Museum

State Capitol

to Stone Mountain
Park →

Turner Field

Martin Luther King Jr.
Birthplace

Zoo
Atlanta

Atlanta Cyclorama

RALPH DAVID ABERNATHY EXPWY.

M.L. KING JR. DR.

MARIETTA ST.

SOUTH EXPWY.

NORTH EXPWY.

W. PACES FERRY RD.

ATLANTA
& Vicinity

The state capitol building was modeled after the U.S. Capitol building. The main entrance has six large columns with the state seal engraved above them. It opened on July 4, 1889. A total of 1.5 acres of Georgia marble was used for the inside walls and floors. The most striking feature of the capitol is its gold dome, which is 75 feet (23 m) in diameter. The dome is covered with two layers of gold mined in north Georgia. On top of the dome is the Miss Freedom statue that weighs one ton. She holds a sword in one hand and a torch in the other to honor Georgia's soldiers who died in wars.

Downtown Atlanta is where you will find all kinds of stores and businesses. They are located in tall, gleaming skyscrapers. The Peachtree Center complex is a collection of office towers, stores, and convention centers. The buildings are connected by tunnels and skywalks.

Across the railroad tracks from the site of the original Western & Atlantic terminal is Underground Atlanta. The front entrance is a thirteen-story light tower. Underground there are more than three hundred shops and restaurants. Above ground, you can visit the CNN Center to see how

Underground Atlanta has many shops and restaurants.

Action seems nonstop
in the CNN newsroom.

news is broadcast. You can also sit in the audience for a talk show. The escalator in the building zips up eighty floors.

In the middle of the downtown area is Centennial Olympic Park. Thousands of people gave money to build the park where many people gathered during the 1996 Olympic Games. If you look at the bricks in the walkways throughout the park, you will see the names of people who gave money. At the Ring Fountain you can play in the cool water spray. As the jets of water come out of the fountain they form five interlocking Olympic rings. It is one of the world's largest fountains, with 251 water jets.

Near a section of Atlanta called Little Five Points, you will find the Jimmy Carter Library and Presidential Center. The library holds many important papers from President Carter's time in the White House (1977–1981). There are 27 million pages of information plus 1.5

million photos there. You can even see the former President's sixth-grade report card!

The Sweet Auburn area of Atlanta is where Dr. Martin Luther King Jr. was born. You can visit the house he lived in until he was twelve years old. Dr. King's grave is at Freedom Plaza. He is buried in a crypt made of white marble at the center of a reflecting pool.

Historical reminders are all over the city. The Atlanta History Center presents the history of the city, the Civil War, and crafts made by Georgians. In Grant Park, the Cyclorama is an important stop. This is the world's largest painting. Eleven artists worked on it in the 1890s. Called the "Battle of Atlanta," the painting is a giant cylinder 42 feet (13 m) high and 358 feet (109 m) around. The cylinder revolves, showing the story of the battle scene by scene.

You can sample many flavors of Coke at the World of Coca-Cola Museum.

The World of Coca-Cola Museum is a three-story building where you'll discover the history of this popular soft drink. Drop in at Club Coca-Cola and sample thirty-eight kinds of Coke, some of which are not sold in the United States.

Atlanta has many other wonders. Check out Zoo Atlanta to see more than 1,000 animals in their natural habitats. One of the most popular exhibits is the rain forest with gorillas. The Margaret Mitchell House and

The figures of Jefferson Davis, Stonewall Jackson, and Robert E. Lee are carved into the granite of Stone Mountain.

Museum is another stop. This is the home where Margaret Mitchell lived while she wrote *Gone with the Wind*. At the Fernback Museum of Natural History, you can see displays that trace the history of the state from dinosaur days to the present. Take a look at Argentinosaurus, the largest dinosaur skeleton ever uncovered. Also closeby is Atlanta Botanical Garden, which features tropical, desert, and endangered plants from around the world. The SciTrek—the Science and Technology Museum of Atlanta—is one of the top ten science centers in the United States. Here, you can lift a car engine with one hand or hear someone whisper from eighty feet (24 m) away.

Just outside Atlanta is Stone Mountain Park. This park covers more than 3,200 acres. Here, you'll find the world's largest bas-relief sculpture. It is carved from a huge area of granite in the side of the mountain. The sculpture shows three leaders of the Confederacy—Jefferson Davis, General Stonewall Jackson, and General Robert E. Lee. Not far from Atlanta is Kennesaw Mountain National Battlefield Park. This huge park honors one of the battlefields in General Sherman's attack on Atlanta. You can hike the trails or picnic in the park.

Wind up your tour of Atlanta at Six Flags Over Georgia. Take a ride on the Georgia Scorcher. This roller coaster offers 3,000 feet (914 m) of twisting terror and reaches speeds up to fifty-four miles per hour.

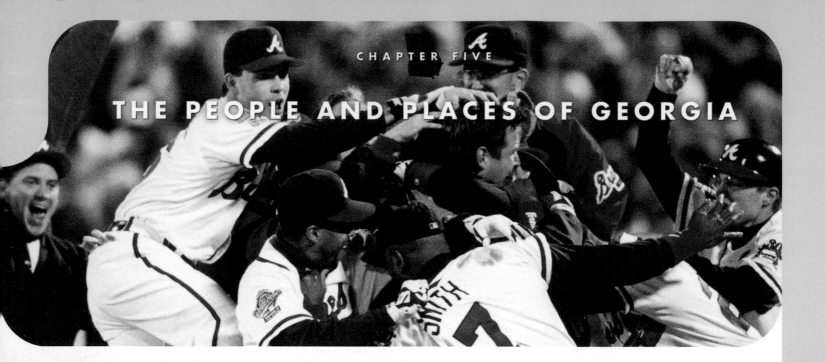

CHAPTER FIVE

THE PEOPLE AND PLACES OF GEORGIA

The Atlanta Braves celebrate winning the World Series in 1995.

Georgians are world famous for their southern hospitality and warm smiles. Throughout the state, many towns host harvest festivals and cultural events. For example, Cherokee Country has an annual weekend honoring Native Americans. The St. Patrick's Day Parade in Savannah is the second largest in the nation, next to the parade in New York City. One of the biggest fairs in Georgia is the Georgia National Fair in Perry. It promotes the state's people, heritage, and agriculture.

MEET THE PEOPLE

The 2000 U.S. Census revealed that more than eight million people live in Georgia. It is the tenth largest state in the United States. The Census also showed that between 1990 and 2000, Georgia gained more people than any other state except California, Texas, and Florida. Georgia was the fastest growing state outside the mountain states of the West.

More than half of Georgia's population lives in or around Atlanta. About seven out of ten Georgians are Caucasian. African-Americans are the largest minority group—they make up more than a quarter of the population. Georgia's Hispanic population has grown by about three hundred percent within the last ten years. About 21,000 Native Americans live in the state. Some of the descendants of the first European settlers still live in Georgia. They came from England, Scotland, Germany, Austria, and Switzerland.

The African heritage is found throughout Georgia. However, it may be strongest on the barrier islands just off the eastern Georgia coast. African-Americans on the Sea Islands are thought to be descended from slaves brought from Angola. The Angolans were called Gullah. Today, Gullah refers to a kind of speech particular to the Sea Islands. African-American towns sprang up near the Ogeechee River.

These people are celebrating the festival of Gold Rush Days at Dahlonega.

WORKING IN GEORGIA

Today, Georgia has many jobs available so that most Georgians can find work. Georgia is the headquarters for many major companies, including Coca-Cola, CNN, Delta Airlines, and United Parcel Sevices. Manufacturing makes up about 20 percent of Georgia's economy. Carpet and rug making and cotton cloth account for the largest amount of manufactured goods. However, paper and wood pulp, food processing, chemical production, and transportation equipment are also important. More paper and board, tufted textile products, and processed chicken are produced in Georgia than anywhere else in the United States. Almost 75 percent of the United States' supply of resins and turpentine comes from Georgia.

Jobs in poultry processing, construction, and carpet-making attract many people from outside the state. Many factories are located near Atlanta or Savannah, including the Lockheed Martin factory in Marietta where fighter jets are made.

About 28 out of 100 Georgians work in offices as lawyers, secretaries, bankers, insurance agents, real estate salespeople, or Web site designers, among other things. Most of the jobs are in the Atlanta area. About one in four people work in stores or malls throughout the state.

The F-22 Tactical Fighter is assembled at the Lockheed Martin factory in Marietta.

About fifteen out of one hundred people work for the state and national government. They are police officers, schoolteachers, and soldiers. Many people work for the U.S. Government on one of the twelve military bases in Georgia, including Fort Benning near Columbus.

There are about 50,000 farms in the state. Georgia's top crops are peanuts, cotton, peaches, and pecans. Georgia produces more pecans than does any other state. One unusual vegetable is the Vidalia onion,

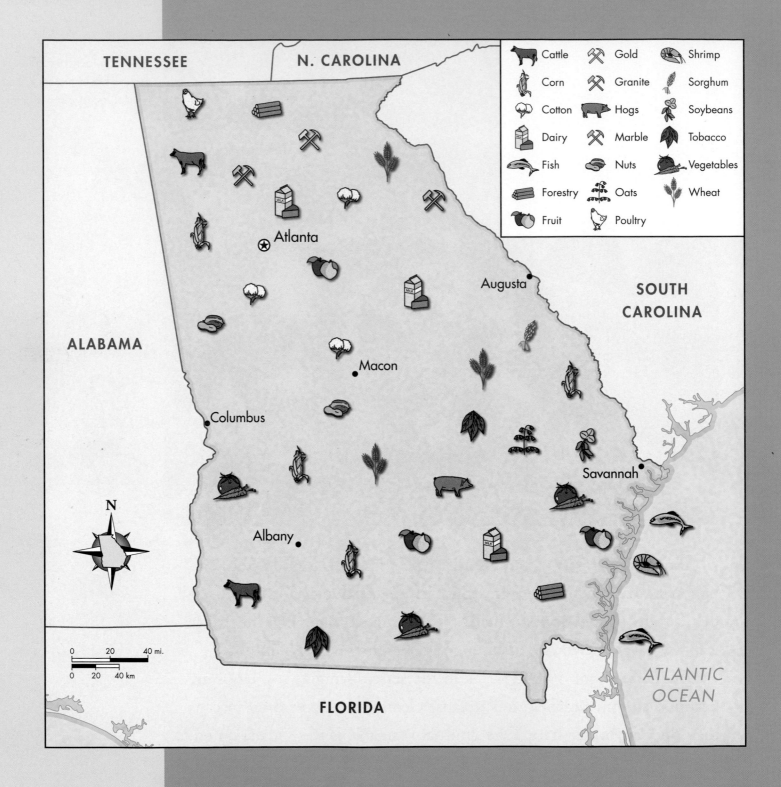

TENNESSEE

N. CAROLINA

ALABAMA

SOUTH CAROLINA

Atlanta

Augusta

Macon

Columbus

Savannah

Albany

FLORIDA

ATLANTIC OCEAN

N

0   20   40 mi.

0   20   40 km

	Cattle		Gold		Shrimp
	Corn		Granite		Sorghum
	Cotton		Hogs		Soybeans
	Dairy		Marble		Tobacco
	Fish		Nuts		Vegetables
	Forestry		Oats		Wheat
	Fruit		Poultry		

Rows and rows of peanuts grow on this farm.

which can only be grown in one area in southeast Georgia. Many people claim this is the sweetest onion in the world. Besides crops, Georgia farms rank second in the nation in chicken production.

There are a few thousand miners in Georgia. Georgia clay is mined and shipped throughout the world. The state is the nation's top producer of kaolin. It is valuable clay that is used to make plastic, paper, paint, rubber, and cat litter. The state is number one in granite mining and also mines limestone. Georgia marble is used in many homes and office buildings.

above left:
This is a granite quarry in Elberton.

above right:
Shrimp fishing is an important industry in Georgia.

Commercial fishers in the coastal towns of Savannah, Brunswick, and Darien catch shrimp, crabs, and oysters from the Atlantic Ocean. Some of the fresh seafood is sold at local markets. The rest is sold to food processing plants. Workers make canned and frozen seafood products that are shipped all over the world.

Tourism is another source of income. About $16.2 billion was made from parks and attractions throughout the state in 2000. Tourism fills hotels and motels, packs restaurants, and provides thousands of jobs.

Georgia ranks third in the nation in peach production. One of the best ways to enjoy sweet, juicy peaches is the cobbler recipe below. Remember to ask an adult for help.

PEACH COBBLER

1 cup of flour
1 cup of sugar
1 stick of margarine
1 cup of milk
Dash of cinnamon
2 cups of fresh peaches, sliced and
    sprinkled with sugar

1. Melt the margarine in a 2-quart dish in the microwave.
2. Mix the flour and sugar together. Add the cinnamon and milk and stir until mixed.
3. Pour this mixture over the margarine.
4. Stir to mix again, then pour the peaches on top.
5. Add a little sugar and cinnamon on top.
6. Cook mixture at 350°F (177°C) for 45 minutes. It should be brown and have a crust.
7. Serve with vanilla ice cream.

Georgia's sandy beaches and barrier islands entice summer visitors. Atlanta is a major attraction all year. Georgia's Stone Mountain Park is the second most popular attraction in the southeast next to Disney World in Orlando, Florida.

TAKE A TOUR OF GEORGIA

Southeast Georgia

Savannah, at the mouth of the Savannah River on the Atlantic coast, is a good place to start your tour. It is a major seaport. Savannah's people work in shipping, paper making, food processing, and plastics. The largest employer is the U.S. Government with a huge military base at nearby Fort Stewart.

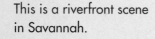

This is a riverfront scene in Savannah.

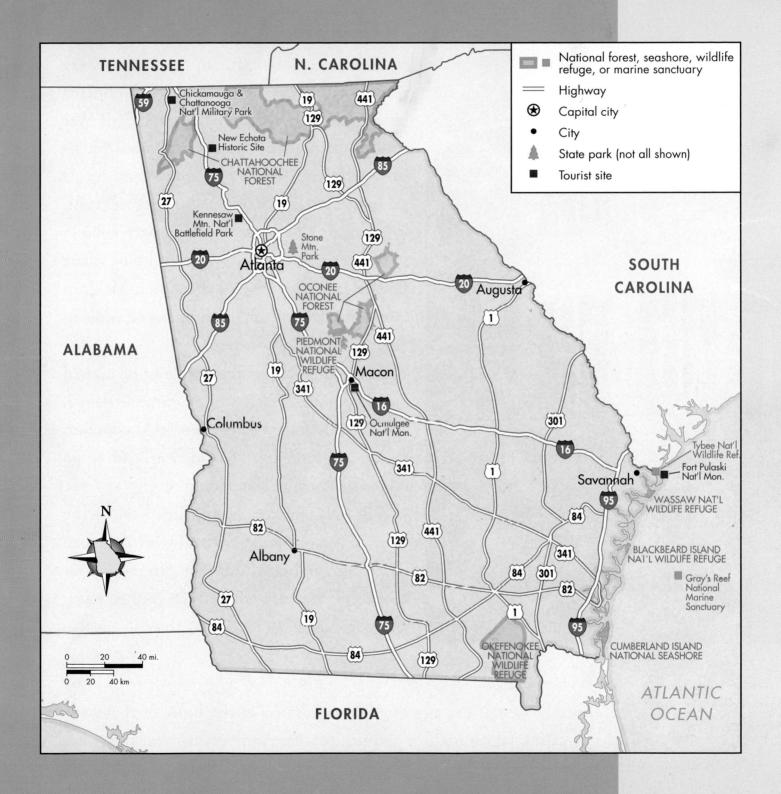

TENNESSEE

N. CAROLINA

SOUTH CAROLINA

ALABAMA

FLORIDA

ATLANTIC OCEAN

Chickamauga & Chattanooga Nat'l Military Park

New Echota Historic Site

CHATTAHOOCHEE NATIONAL FOREST

Kennesaw Mtn. Nat'l Battlefield Park

Stone Mtn. Park

Atlanta

OCONEE NATIONAL FOREST

Augusta

PIEDMONT NATIONAL WILDLIFE REFUGE

Macon

Ocmulgee Nat'l Mon.

Columbus

Albany

Savannah

Tybee Nat'l Wildlife Ref.

Fort Pulaski Nat'l Mon.

WASSAW NAT'L WILDLIFE REFUGE

BLACKBEARD ISLAND NAT'L WILDLIFE REFUGE

Gray's Reef National Marine Sanctuary

CUMBERLAND ISLAND NATIONAL SEASHORE

OKEFENOKEE NATIONAL WILDLIFE REFUGE

N

0   20   40 mi.
0   20   40 km

National forest, seashore, wildlife refuge, or marine sanctuary

Highway

Capital city

City

State park (not all shown)

Tourist site

63

The Andrew Low house is where Juliette Low grew up.

Tourism is important to Savannah. Every year crowds of people come to see Savannah's historic district, old churches, and Civil War cotton warehouses. The city is famous for its streets that are designed in squares and for its gardens. Most of the original squares still exist.

You can take a carriage ride over cobblestone streets. You can also visit the home where Juliette Low grew up, or the Green-Meldrim House where General Sherman stayed while in Savannah.

Many families spend time at resorts located on the popular beaches of St. Simons, Jekyll, and Tybee Islands. Visitors rent Jet Skis and eat fresh seafood. People can ride on boats to go deep-sea fishing or watch dolphins.

The Okefenokee Swamp lies west of the coast. It is a protected wetland with alligators, bears, deer, and rare birds. You can take a tour boat to view these wild creatures in their natural environment.

Central Georgia

Further west is the city of Albany. Located in the heart of the state's farmland, farms produce peanuts, peaches, and pecans. Near the city is the Parks at Chehaw, a drive-through wild animal park where you can see animals of the African savannah.

To the northwest, you can stop at Plains, the hometown of President Jimmy Carter. Not far from there is Andersonville National Historic Site where more than 45,000 Union troops were kept in prison during the Civil War. More than 12,000 soldiers died because of a lack of shelter, food, and medical supplies.

Not far from Plains is Providence Canyon. The canyon has sixteen narrow valleys with drops of over 150 feet (46 m). There are forty different kinds of soil within the canyon walls. Each kind of soil has a different color ranging from deep lilac to white as sugar.

Columbus is located on the border of Alabama on the Chattahoochee River. It is Georgia's second largest city. Columbus is located near Fort Benning, a major Army base. Columbus is a textile center for producing

Providence Canyon State Park has narrow and deep valleys.

cotton cloth. Other city industries process peanuts, make soft drinks, build machinery, and refine metals.

Downtown Columbus is a national historic district. The area covers twenty-eight square blocks and features many old homes. The Springer Opera House was built in 1871 and is the official State Theatre of Georgia. Plays and musicals are often presented there. You can take a walking tour of the city and see a trader's cabin, a farm, and the Pemberton House, where Coca-Cola was invented. There is a new twelve-mile riverwalk along the Chattahoochee River. The Convention and Trade Center is in an old factory where bullets and canons were made during the Civil War. You could also take a ride on a riverboat dating from the 1880s.

Macon lies in the central part of the state. The city's nickname is the "Heart of Georgia" because of its location. During the 1800s, Macon was at the center of the cotton region. You can visit some of the large plantations around the city. Macon is noted for its cherry trees. There are 200,000 cherry trees around the city. Every March, the city hosts an International Cherry Blossom Festival where you'll find plenty of music, food, and fun.

Macon also has several museums and halls of fame. At the Georgia Sports Hall of Fame, you can play video golf or try racing in a NASCAR car. At the Museum of Arts and Sciences you can see the skeleton of a 40-million-year-old whale and view the stars in a planetarium. Visit the Georgia Music Hall of Fame to learn about many fine musicians and entertainers who have come from Georgia, including James Brown and Otis Redding.

The city of Augusta started as a fur trading post on the Savannah River. Every April the best professional golfers from the United States and other countries come to Augusta to play in the Masters Golf Tournament on the Augusta National Golf Course. It is known as one of the most beautiful courses in the world, and the tournament is considered one of the best.

North Georgia

Athens is northwest of Augusta. The city is home to the University of Georgia. On the town square is the world's only double-barreled

Macon's cherry trees produce beautiful blossoms in the spring.

This is a dazzling view of Atlanta's skyline.

cannon. It was made during the Civil War, but the inventor could not get it to work properly. The original constitution of the Confederate States of America is on display at the university's library.

To the west is the state's capital and largest city—Atlanta. It is the business center of the southeast. Hartsfield Atlanta International Airport is the busiest airport in the world. The city's skyline is lined with new skyscrapers. Four professional sporting teams play baseball, football, hockey, and

WHO'S WHO IN GEORGIA?

Ted Turner (1938–) is a self-made billionaire who started several cable television stations including TBS, CNN, and Cartoon Network. He owns several professional sports teams—the Atlanta Braves, Atlanta Hawks, and Atlanta Thrashers.

Just north of Atlanta, the Chattahoochee flows through the wilderness.

basketball in Atlanta. In 1995, the Atlanta Braves won the World Series Championship.

Beyond Atlanta and nestled within the mountains are many beautiful natural attractions, including waterfalls and steep mountain trails. Small towns are scattered throughout the hills.

GEORGIA ALMANAC

Statehood date and number: January 2, 1788/fourth

State seal (date adopted): adopted 1799, revised 1914

State flag (date adopted): 2001

Geographic center: Twiggs, 18 miles southeast of Macon

Total area/rank: 58,977 square miles (152,750 sq km)/24th

Coastline/rank: 100 miles (161 km)/18th

Borders: Tennessee, North Carolina, South Carolina, Alabama, Florida, and the Atlantic Ocean

Latitude and longitude: Georgia is located approximately between 35° 00' and 30° 42' N and 80° 53' and 85° 36' W.

Highest/lowest elevation: Brasstown Bald Mountain, 4,784 feet (1,458 km)/sea level

Hottest/coldest temperature: 113° F (45° C) in Greenville on May 27, 1978/–17° F (–27° C) in Floyd County on January 27, 1940

Land area/rank: 57,919 square miles (150,010 sq km)/21st

Inland water: 1,522 square miles (3,940 sq km)

Population/rank: 8,186,453 (2000 Census)/10th

Population of major cities: (2000 Census) Atlanta (416,474), Augusta-Richmond County (199,775), Columbus (186,291), Savannah (131,510), Athens-Clarke County (101,489), and Macon (97,255)

Origin of state name: King George II of England

State capital: Atlanta

Previous capitals: Savannah, Augusta, Louisville, Milledgeville, and Macon

Counties: 159

State government: 56 senators; 180 representatives

Major rivers/lakes: Altamaha, Savannah, and Chattahoochee/Lanier, Allatoona, and Hartwell

Farm products: Peanuts, cotton, pecans, and poultry

Livestock: Cattle, hogs/pigs, chickens

Manufactured products: Carpet, Coca-Cola, food processing, poultry processing

Mining products: Marble, mica, barite, granite, kaolin, sand, and fuller's earth

Fishing products: Shrimp, crabs, and oysters

Bird: Brown Thrasher

Flower: Cherokee Rose

Fossil: Shark tooth

Motto: "Wisdom, Justice and Moderation"

Nicknames: Empire State of the South, Peach State

Song: "Georgia on My Mind"

Tree: Live oak

Vegetable: Vidalia sweet onion

TIME**LINE**

Hernando de Soto leads first exploration of Georgia

Slaves begin to be sold for plantation labor

Gold is discovered

Georgia joins the Confederate States of America

James Oglethorpe and colonists establish Savannah

About 40,000 people live in Georgia

Eli Whitney invents cotton gin

Cherokees march on the "Trail of Tears"

Sherman's troops burn a path to Savannah

British forces capture Savannah

| 1540 | 1733 | 1750 | 1776 | 1778 | 1793 | 1828 | 1838 | 1861 | 1864 |

| 1607 | 1620 | 1776 | 1783 | 1787 | 1812–15 | 1843 | 1846–48 | 1861–65 |

The first permanent British settlement at Jamestown, Virginia

American Revolutionary War ends

Pioneers travel west on the Oregon Trail

Pilgrims set up Plymouth colony

U.S. Constitution is written

U.S. fights war with Mexico

American colonies declare independence from England

U.S. and England fight the War of 1812

Civil War occurs in the United States

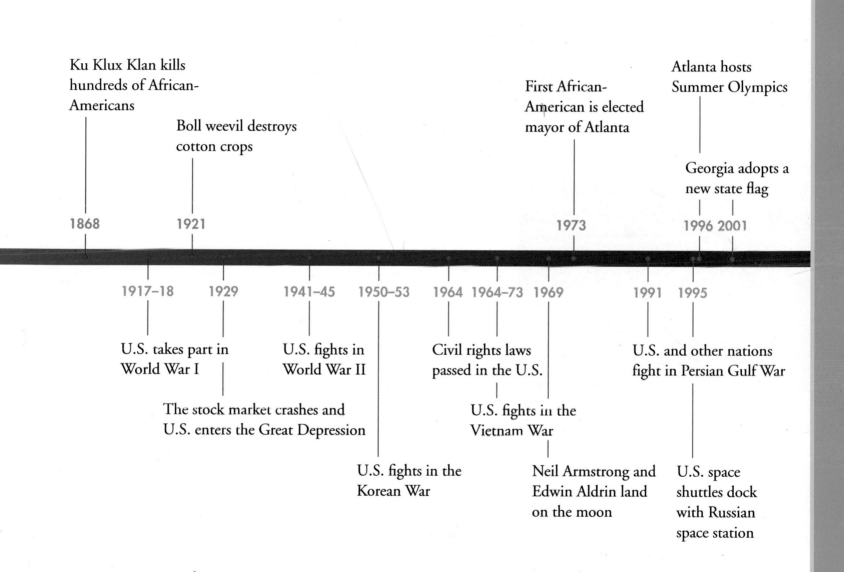

Ku Klux Klan kills
hundreds of African-
Americans

Boll weevil destroys
cotton crops

First African-
American is elected
mayor of Atlanta

Atlanta hosts
Summer Olympics

Georgia adopts a
new state flag

1868   1921   1973   1996 2001

1917–18   1929   1941–45   1950–53   1964 1964–73 1969   1991 1995

U.S. takes part in
World War I

U.S. fights in
World War II

Civil rights laws
passed in the U.S.

U.S. and other nations
fight in Persian Gulf War

The stock market crashes and
U.S. enters the Great Depression

U.S. fights in the
Vietnam War

U.S. fights in the
Korean War

Neil Armstrong and
Edwin Aldrin land
on the moon

U.S. space
shuttles dock
with Russian
space station

GALLERY OF FAMOUS GEORGIANS

Jimmy Carter
(1924–)
Elected as the 39th president of the United States. Born in Plains.

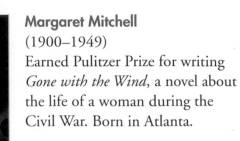

Ray Charles
(1930–)
Legendary singer who has won many awards, including twelve Grammy awards. Born in Albany.

Ty Cobb
(1886–1961)
Known as the "Georgia Peach," he was one of major league baseball's best players and fiercest competitors. Born in Narrows.

Dr. Martin Luther King Jr.
(1929–1968)
Leader of the Civil Rights movement in the 1960s. Born in Atlanta.

Margaret Mitchell
(1900–1949)
Earned Pulitzer Prize for writing *Gone with the Wind*, a novel about the life of a woman during the Civil War. Born in Atlanta.

Jackie Robinson
(1919–1972)
First African-American to play major league baseball, later voted into the Hall of Fame. Born in Cairo.

Alexander Hamilton Stephens
(1812–1883)
Served as vice president of the Confederacy and 25 years in the U.S. Congress. Born in Taliaferro County.

Clarence Thomas
(1948–)
A justice on the U.S. Supreme Court. Born in Pin Point.

Wyomia Tyus
(1945–)
A sprinter who was the first to win a gold medal for the same event in two Olympic games. Born in Griffin.

Alice Walker
(1944–)
Novelist and poet. Author of *The Color Purple* and *Meridian*. Born in Eatonton.

GLOSSARY

appeal: to ask a higher court to review a lower court decision

assassinate: to attack and kill an important person

barrier islands: a group of islands next to the coastline

census: official government count of population

constitution: the basic laws and principles under which a country, state, or organization is governed

Ku Klux Klan: secret society formed to oppose African-Americans and other groups

legislature: group of people elected to make laws

peat: a sponge-like layer of ground made from decayed and dried plants

plantation: a large farm on which crops are grown

rebels: people who fight against or resist a government or authority

refuge: a protected area

secede: to withdraw or separate from something

segregation: the act of keeping people of different races separate

sharecropper: a person who rents farmland or shares harvest profits with a landowner

treaty: an agreement between two governments that they both must obey

veto: the ability to reject a law passed by the legislature

FOR MORE INFORMATION

Web sites

About North Georgia
www.ngeorgia.com
Historical and tourist information about North Georgia.

Carl Vinson Institute of Government
The University of Georgia
www.cviog.uga.edu/Projects/gainfo/contents.htm
Contains historical, cultural, and political information.

State of Georgia
www.state.ga.us/
Links to all the state government agencies and elected officials.

Books

Bruchac, Joseph and Diana Magnuson. *The Trail of Tears,* New York: Random Library, 1999.

Hakim, Joy. *The First Americans: Prehistory–1600*, New York: Oxford University Press Children's Books, 1999.

Lester, Julius, and Tom Feelings. *To Be a Slave*, New York: Scholastic Paperbacks, 1988.

Moore, Kay, and Anni Matsick. *If You Lived at the Time of the Civil War*, New York: Scholastic Trade, 1994.

Tate, Eleanora. *Thank You, Dr. Martin Luther King, Jr.!* Yearling Books, 1992.

Addresses

Georgia House of Representatives
Public Information Office
Room 131, State Capitol 30334

Georgia Department of Industry, Trade, and Tourism
285 Peachtree Center Avenue, NE
Marquis Two Tower, Suite 1000
Atlanta, GA 30303-1230

INDEX

ABOUT THE AUTHOR

Pattie Stechschulte graduated from the University of Toledo in 1988. She has been a professional writer for more than eleven years in the areas of health care, children, and sports. She has received several awards for her writing. She lives in Marietta, Georgia, with her two young sons and husband.